Ask a question to

the magic book

It will answer

you ...

The Magic Book is your guide to spirituality.

It will allow you to let your intuition guide you to the answers you need.

Ask your question in a low voice and think for a few moments while resting your hand on the book.

Scroll through the pages without looking for a few seconds and stop

when your stop when your instinct
tells you that your answer is there.
Like all divinatory arts **The**
Magic Book *requires practice and*
reflection.

We wish you a safe journey into the
mysteries of the unknown.

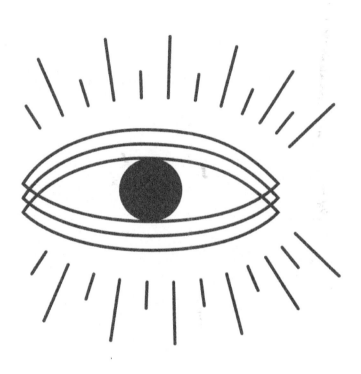

You know the truth deep down. Accept to see what you are hiding.

Definitely.

Not at all.

You will soon find happy days. For after the rain comes the good weather.

At first sight,

no.

This time will

be the right

time.

The book is waiting for more relevant questions.

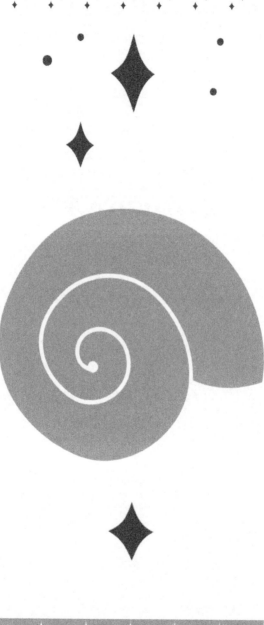

The book is

certain of this !

The greatest

strength is not

in the conflict.

Put this subject

aside.

I have no

opinion on this.

It is likely.

Nothing is

impossible.

Success awaits

you.

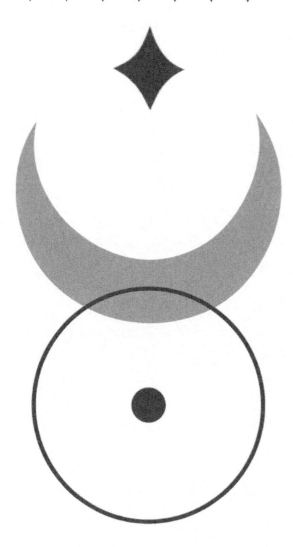

A time for everything. The first step is to find yourself.

This initiative

will prove

beneficial.

Yes, it says.

Of course.

Almost.

Absolutely.

Love is the greatest medicine and it cannot be bought.

It will be

harder than you

think.

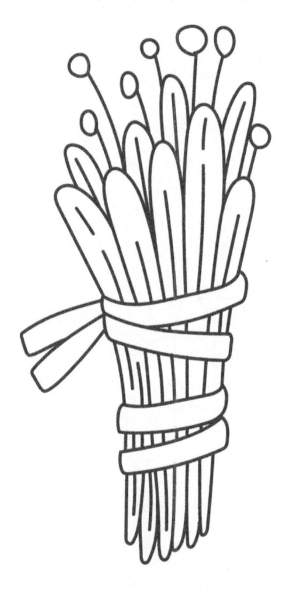

Redouble your efforts for what you want to achieve.

You have the strength within you. No one will stop you.

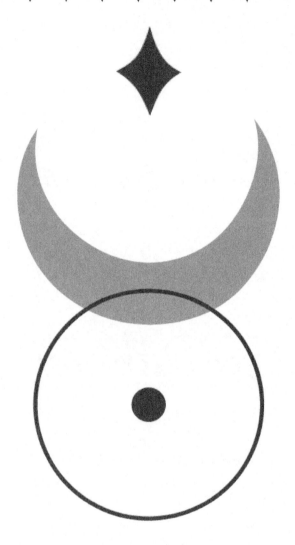

Without a

doubt !

If everything goes according to plan, you have a chance !

Rephrase your

question.

A little more concentration is what you need.

Of course.

Yes, the alignment of Mercury and the Sun protects you on this path.

There are

answers that are

better left

unheard.

Not in the

near future.

There is
nothing you can
do to prevent
what must
happen.

Certainly.

Definitely !

There is a
beginning to all
great things.
You are on
the right path.

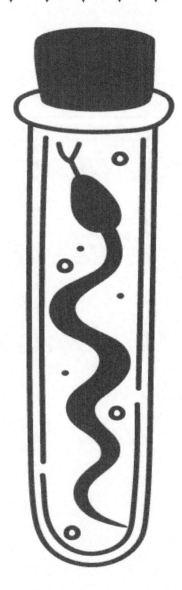

The cure is

worse than the

disease.

Don't do this.

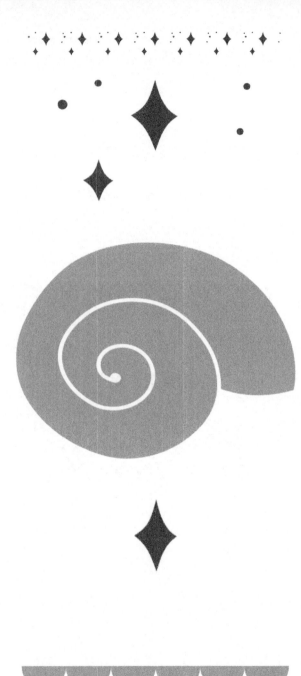

Yes !!

Fortune

favours the bold.

The stars are

aligned in your

favour.

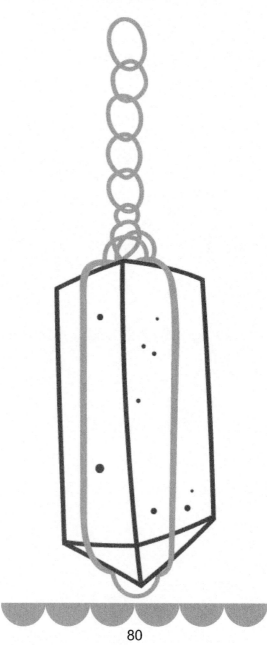

It's not just up

to you.

Your request is

not feasible.

Your desire is accessible. But be more ambitious in the future.

One day yes,

but not today.

Yes !

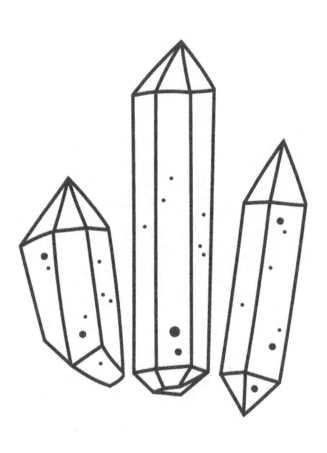

Keep hope.

Focus on

another subject.

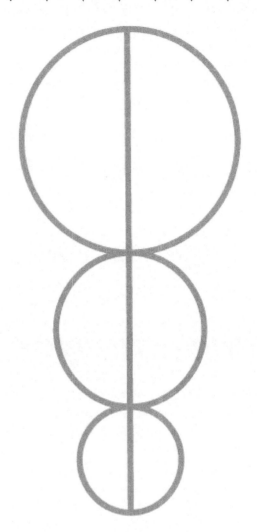

Yes, your

excellent

initiative will be

successful.

Not at all.

Possible.

Yes, but you will have to try harder.

I have no

opinion on this.

It is likely !

Nothing is

impossible.

You have all

the resources you

need.

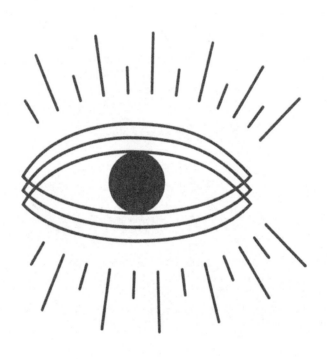

Never.

Try something

else.

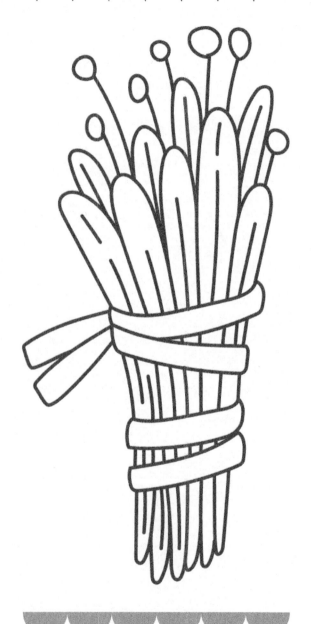

Redouble your efforts for what you want to achieve.

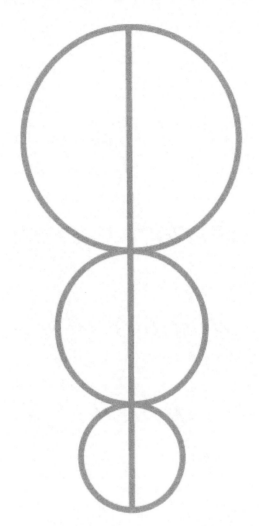

I believe it is

possible !

You will still

have to be

patient. But it

will happen.

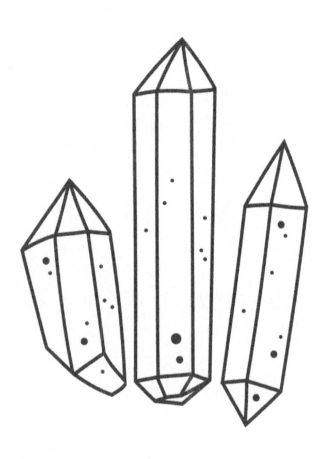

You are on the right path. Your initiative will be successful.

I am

pessimistic about

this.

No.

Yes.

It is conceivable.

Your request can

be fulfilled by your

presence of mind

and your harmony

with this book.

I have no

opinion on this.

Yes, there will be hardships but your determination will make the difference.

Nothing is

impossible.

Not this time.

Ask the book

again

tomorrow.

Yes, totally!

The alignment of Mars with Mercury offers a protective sky in this endeavour.

In any case.

Yes, it is

written.

Of course.

Almost.

Absolutely.

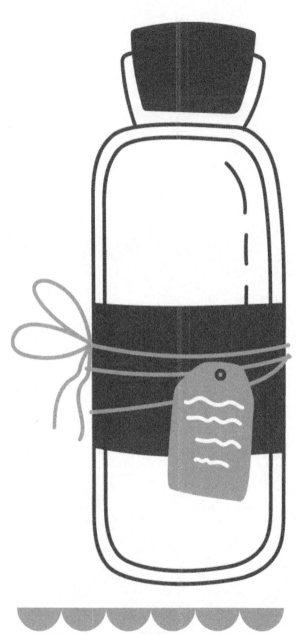

Have hope !

Yes, but you

will have to be

brave.

Work hard for what you want to achieve. Only your determination will make a difference.

Definitely not. This is not the right way.

Yes. Your

happiness is

foretold.

There is a

chance.

This requires

reflection.

Yes.

Sometimes.

The answer is

no.

This may be the

case.

Yes !

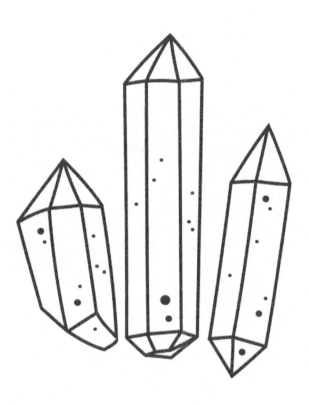

I don't know.

That's right.

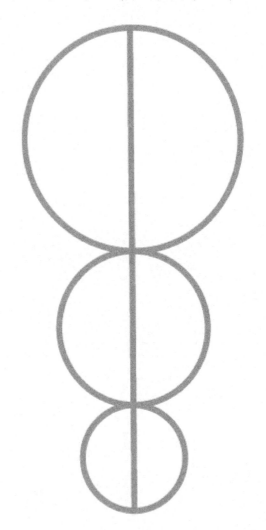

Yes.

Not at all.

Possible.

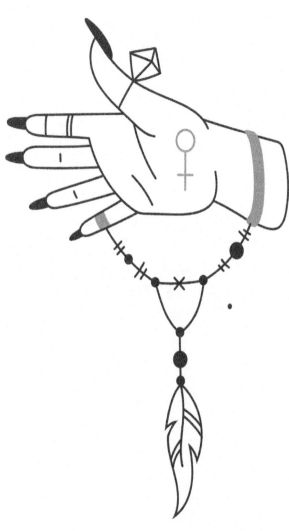

Possibly.

I have no

opinion on this.

This is likely.

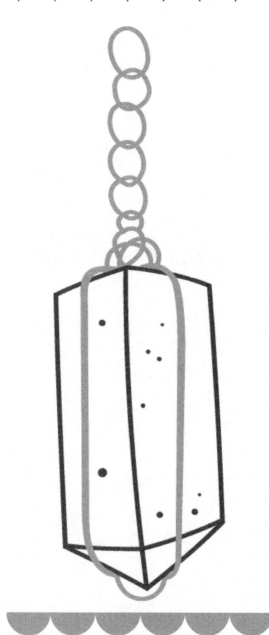

The whole

universe says

yes !

Printed in Great Britain
by Amazon

13310001R00108